Ripley's Believe It or Not!®

Developed and produced by Ripley Publishing Ltd

This edition published and distributed by:

Mason Crest
370 Reed Road, Broomall, Pennsylvania 19008
www.masoncrest.com

Printed and bound in the United States of America.

First printing
9 8 7 6 5 4 3 2 1

Ripley's Believe It or Not!
Epic Endeavors
ISBN-13: 978-1-4222-2568-4 (hardcover)
ISBN-13: 978-1-4222-9243-3 (e-book)
Ripley's Believe It or Not!—Complete 16 Title Series
ISBN-13: 978-1-4222-2560-8

Library of Congress Cataloging-in-Publication Data

Epic endeavors.
    p. cm. — (Ripley's believe it or not!)
ISBN 978-1-4222-2568-4 (hardcover) — ISBN 978-1-4222-2560-8 (series hardcover) —
ISBN 978-1-4222-9243-3 (ebook)
1. Voyages and travels—Juvenile literature. 2. Curiosities and wonders—Juvenile literature.
G570.P73 2012
910.4—dc23
                    2012020340

PUBLISHER'S NOTE
While every effort has been made to verify the accuracy of the entries in this book, the Publisher's cannot be held responsible for any errors contained in the work. They would be glad to receive any information from readers.

WARNING
Some of the stunts and activities in this book are undertaken by experts and should not be attempted by anyone without adequate training and supervision.

Ripley's Believe It or Not!®

Disbelief and Shock!

EPIC ENDEAVORS

www.MasonCrest.com

EPIC ENDEAVORS

Reaching the limit. Be astounded at the amazing adventures, extreme challenges, and startling successes inside this book. Meet the man who dodged pirates to swim the Amazon River, the artist who can draw intricate buildings from memory, and the escapologist who spent 10 minutes 17 seconds chained and handcuffed underwater.

Kent Couch flew over Oregon on a chair held up by helium-filled balloons.

COUCH BALLOON

Kent Couch flew nearly 200 mi (322 km) over Oregon in nine hours in July 2007—in a contraption that consisted of nothing more than a lawn chair and 105 brightly colored, helium-filled balloons.

Inspired by Larry "Lawn Chair" Walters, who floated over Los Angeles, California, using weather balloons in 1982, the 47-year-old attached the bundle of 4-ft-round (1.2-m) balloons to his chair and took off from his gas station in Bend, Oregon. He carried a global-positioning device, a two-way radio, a digital camcorder, a cell phone, and a pair of sunglasses.

He also had instruments to measure his altitude and speed, plus four plastic bags, each holding 5 gal (19 l) of water, to act as ballast. To increase altitude, he simply released some of the water.

He traveled as high as 14,000 ft (4,267 m) as he floated eastward and said he could hear cattle and children as he drifted among the clouds. On the ground below, friends and family followed his progress in a convoy of vehicles.

His intended destination was Idaho, but with his water supply running low and mountains approaching, he decided to touch down in a field near Union, Oregon. He completed the descent by popping the balloons.

Afterward, Couch said he would love to do it again. "When you're laying in the grass on a summer day, and you see the clouds, you wish you could jump on them. This is as close as you can come to jumping on them. It was just like being on ice, nice and smooth."

HOW HIGH?

Jet airplanes	35,000 ft
Mt. Everest	29,000 ft
Mt. McKinley	20,000 ft
Kent Couch	14,000 ft
Bald eagles	10,000 ft

Ripley's ask

"Where did your childhood dream of flying by balloon cluster come from? I believe my childhood dream came from a time when I was a kid at a birthday party and was asked to hold a cluster of helium-filled birthday balloons. I could feel the tug on my arm as they wanted to ascend to sky. I remember thinking if I only had a few more I could fly!

What did you fill the balloons up with in your 2007 ride? I used helium.

How long were you flying for? I flew for eight hours and 45 minutes.

Did you have any wobbly moments? Yes I did have two wobbly moments, one when I crossed a mountain range which had some wind vortices that were colliding with each other, making the balloons and chair kinda dance. The other time was when I was reaching out to retrieve a few balloons and my chair wanted to tip to the side I was leaning towards.

What is your most memorable moment of the flight? I think probably the most memorable moment in my flight was at about 14,000 ft looking down at the blue mountain range. For a moment, I felt so separated from the earth. It was just something about no noise, no people, relaxed in a lawn chair looking down at God's handiwork. Words have a hard time describing my feelings.

Was the balloon couch uncomfortable? The chair was pretty comfortable; however, I don't think I ever sat in one spot for that long. I wiggled around as much as possible.

How did you come back down to earth? I came back to earth by popping balloons one by one until I was satisfied with my descent rate.

Would you do it again? I would definitely do it again if the opportunity arises."

RUNS IN FAMILY

Thirteen sons and daughters of Janet Weisse of Oshkosh, Wisconsin—aged between 33 and 54—took part in the 2007 Fox Cities Marathon at Appleton. All 13 completed the course.

SPEEDY SOFA

A gardener from London, England, hit speeds of 92 mph (148 km/h) in May 2007—driving a sofa! Marek Turowski demonstrated the go-faster furniture at an airfield in Leicestershire. The rear-engined, street legal, high-speed sofa was built by Edd China, who has also designed an 87 mph (140 km/h) office desk.

MARATHON EFFORT

Richard Takata of Toronto, Ontario, Canada, ran a marathon on seven different continents in just under 30 days in 2007. He took part in marathons in New Zealand, the United States, Egypt, Spain, Antarctica, Argentina, and Cyprus. Before his first race he had more than a foot of hair cut off that had taken him four years to grow.

WATERFALL PLUNGE

Tyler Bradt, 21, of Missoula, Montana, successfully paddled his kayak over a thunderous 107-ft (33-m) waterfall in September 2007. He made the daring drop at the Alexandra Falls on the Hay River in Canada's Northwest Territories—and landed at the bottom without flipping, even though part of the cockpit of his kayak exploded on impact.

CLIMBING FANATIC

Cheered on by 200 supporters, an Indian man scaled a 2,100-ft (640-m) hill 101 times in the space of 20 hours in August 2007. Bank employee Girish Kulkarni from Pune has been practicing running up hills for five years.

MOUNTAIN DASH

Austria's Marcus Stoeckl, aged 33, reached a speed of 130.7 mph (210 km/h) while traveling down a snow-covered mountain in Chile—on a mountain bike—in September 2007. His icy dash made him the fastest man on two wheels without an engine.

NONSTOP RIDE

George Hood, of Aurora, Illinois, rode a stationary bike nonstop for nearly five days in 2007. He finally stopped pedaling at 111 hours 11 minutes 11 seconds because the time was easy to remember. He said that he started having hallucinations about eating donuts toward the end of his multi-marathon ride.

SUBWAY SPRINT

Armed only with beef jerky and water, college friends Don Badaczewski and Matt Green rode the entire New York subway system nonstop in just over 24 hours in August 2006. They set off from Queens and finished in the Bronx after passing through all 468 stations on the city's 26 lines... with no bathroom breaks. Don had the idea for the underground adventure after reading about riding the subway on the Internet.

EPIC ADVENTURE

Using only human power, Colin Angus of Vancouver Island, British Columbia, Canada, circumnavigated the world in 720 days between 2004 and 2006. Starting and finishing in Vancouver, he cycled, skied, canoed, walked, and rowed through 17 countries, going through around 4,000 chocolate bars, 550 lb (250 kg) of freeze-dried foods, and 72 bicycle inner tubes. He hiked 3,125 mi (5,000 km) across Siberia, was blown 375 miles (600 km) off course while traversing the treacherous Bering Strait and, together with his fiancée Julie Wafaei, rowed for five months across the Atlantic Ocean.

ISLAND SWIM

Skip Storch from New York City spent nearly a day and a half in the water swimming around Manhattan Island in August 2007. He eventually completed three laps of the island in just under 33 hours. Once out of New York's Hudson River, Storch was taken to a hospital to be treated for hypothermia.

WORLD TOUR

From 2001 to 2005, Alastair Humphreys of Yorkshire, England, peddled the world on his bike, riding 45,000 mi (72,420 km) through 60 countries on five continents.

COAST TO COAST

New Yorker Alexander Roy drove the 2,794 mi (4,496 km) from New York City to Los Angeles in October 2006 in just 31 hours 4 minutes. He averaged 90 mph (145 km/h) in his BMW M5, occasionally hitting top speeds of 150 mph (240 km/h).

UNICYCLE MARATHON

Sam Wakeling, a 22-year-old student at Aberystwyth University in Wales, traveled 282 mi (455 km) on a unicycle in a single day in September 2007. The computer science undergraduate was so at home riding his customized unicycle, with 36-in (90-cm) wheels around the university's running track that he covered the first 105 mi (170 km) without dismounting. He eventually completed 1,141 laps at an average speed of nearly 13 mph (21 km/h). In 2005, he had ridden a one-wheeler from the most southwesterly point of England (Land's End) to the northeastern tip of Scotland (John O'Groats)—a distance of 874 mi (1,406 km).

Tuk to the Road

"We stopped at a salt lake in Xinjiang, northwest China, for a few hours of relaxation—the salty water making us look like this!"

Two British women drove a little pink tuk-tuk (a three-wheeled motorized taxi, popular in Thailand) 12,000 mi (19,000 km) through 12 countries from Thailand to England in 2006. Antonia Bolingbroke-Kent and Jo Huxster, both 27, took three months to complete the journey in their tuk-tuk.

Raising money for charity, they traveled through Thailand, Laos, China, Kazakhstan, Russia, Ukraine, Poland, the Czech Republic, Germany, Belgium, and France before finally reaching England. En route they passed such sights as the Great Wall of China and the Gobi Desert.

Although they had to repair two snapped accelerator cables and a failed suspension, the three-wheeler, with a top speed of 70 mph (115 km/h), stood up well to the test and averaged 150 mi (240 km) a day.

Huxster had thought up the idea for the adventure four years earlier during a visit to Thailand. "I was just driving around Bangkok with two friends, and the tuk-tuk driver let me sit in the front to pretend I was driving. I thought, 'One day I will drive one of these back to England.' And that's how it happened."

Wandering sheep were just one of the problems the women had to deal with on their drive across Asia.

Antonia (left) and Jo back in England with their trusty tuk-tuk which they named Ting Tong.

MOSHI MOSHI

EYE OF THE TIGER

Instead of being on the outside of a cage looking in at lions and tigers, Arnd Drossel put himself inside a cage and allowed the big cats to get a close-up. The daring stunt was all part of his 220-mi (355-km) roll through the German state of North-Rhine Westphalia in a ball of steel wire.

The 38-year-old performance artist made his unusual journey to raise money for, and awareness of, mental illness. In fact, psychiatric patients from clinics in the region helped him create the rolling globe, which measured just over 6 ft (1.8 m) in diameter, weighed around 265 lb (120 kg), and was constructed out of 250 bent stainless steel rods. When finished, it resembled a massive ball of steel wool.

Drossel set off in April 2007 from his birthplace of Dorsten and finished his roll-athon in his home town of Warburg. He covered around 13 mi (21 km) a day, propelling the ball by simply shifting his weight in a walking motion. As well as "walking," he ate and slept in the ball. Drossel passed through a number of towns on his journey, but, predictably, his most hair-raising moments occurred in the Stukenbrock Safari Park where he came face to face with the eyes of several tigers, not to mention the lions.

That was when—for the first time in his life—he was happy to be inside a strong, protective cage.

Arnd speeding past the famous Brandenburg Gate in Berlin.

Even a makeshift bed was relaxing for Arnd Drossel after a hard day's walking in his steel globe.

Arnd emerging after a night in his ball.

The journey took him across all kinds of terrain.

The tigers at Germany's Stukenbrock Safari Park are curious about the stranger who has rolled into their paddock.

BAT MAN

A British climber has discovered a new method of tackling tough cliff faces—he hangs upside down like a bat for two minutes while more than 100 ft (30 m) up in the air. Steve McClure from Yorkshire practices the "bat hang" to shake fresh blood back into his arms, thereby ridding them of the crippling lactic acid that builds up during climbs. He created the technique to conquer the treacherous overhang on the 300-ft (90-m) limestone cliff at Malham Cove—one of England's hardest climbs—and after three years and dozens of attempts, "Bat Man" finally reached the top in 2007.

SOLO CROSSING

Michael Perham of Hertfordshire, England, sailed solo across the Atlantic Ocean when he was just 14 years old. The schoolboy set off from Gibraltar in his 28-ft (8.5-m) yacht *Cheeky Monkey* on November 18, 2006, and arrived six and a half weeks later in Antigua in the West Indies on January 3, 2007. During the 3,500-mi (5,635-km) voyage, he had to contend with sharks, technical problems, and ferocious storms.

NAKED AMBITION

In 2007, a couple from Bedfordshire, England, climbed 15 Scottish mountains, each more than 3,000 ft (915 m) in height—naked. The naturists, known only as Stuart and Karla, commemorated each climb with a nude photo of themselves on the summit. There are 284 peaks in Scotland over 3,000 ft—known as the Munros—and Stuart and Karla intend to climb every one.

MULTIPLE JUMPS

In 2006, Jay Stokes of Yuma, Arizona, celebrated his 50th birthday by jumping out of an airplane—640 times. Despite injuring a muscle around the 200th leap, he completed the jumps in 24 hours—averaging out at one jump every 2 minutes 15 seconds.

BLIND ACE

Despite being blinded by diabetes more than 25 years ago, golfer Sheila Drummond hit a hole-in-one at Mahoning Valley Country Club, Lehighton, Pennsylvania, in 2007. The odds of an amateur golfer getting a hole-in-one are 1 in 12,750—for a blind amateur golfer it must be a shot in a million.

CYCLING PHENOMENON

Born with a deformed right leg, Emmanuel Ofosu Yeboah peddled his bike 379 mi (610 km) across Ghana in 2001 using only his left foot in order to challenge stereotypes about the disabled people of his country.

TIGHTROPE WALKER

It took Abudusataer Dujiabudula of China only 11 minutes 22 seconds to walk a half-mile (800-m) tightrope across the Han River in Seoul, South Korea.

JASON'S JOURNEY

British adventurer Jason Lewis completed a 46,000-mi (74,000-km), 13-year journey around the world. Between 1994 and 2007 he walked, cycled, roller-bladed, kayaked, swam, and pedaled across five continents, two oceans, and one sea. En route he was chased by a saltwater crocodile in Australia, questioned as a spy in North Africa, and suffered two fractured legs after being hit by a car in Colorado as he roller-bladed across the United States. To help pay for his adventure, he worked as a cattle drover in North America and in a funeral parlor in Australia.

CROC BAIT

Wearing only a swimming costume, Kerry Shaw was secured inside a reinforced steel cage and plunged into a pool full of 14-ft-long (4-m) crocodiles. She was lowered by crane into position at a wildlife park in Oudtshoom, South Africa, in 2007, and warned that under no circumstances should she reach through the bars!

EXTRA TIME

Two soccer teams at Exeter, Ontario, Canada, played against one another continuously for 30 hours 30 minutes in May 2007. The final score was Stratford Enterprise 138, Exeter Fury 105. Players' injuries included a dislocated shoulder and a broken foot.

HOT WORK

Queensland shearers Dave Grant and Laurie Bateman shaved 709 Merino sheep in just eight hours at Hughenden, Australia, in October 2007. The pair trained for 12 months to build up the stamina necessary for the challenge, during which their bodies perspired up to 135 fl oz (4 l) of sweat every two hours.

UNDERWATER SURVIVOR

Hungarian escape artist David Merlini spent 10 minutes 17 seconds chained and handcuffed underwater in 2007, without air. His hands were tied by five sets of police handcuffs and he was bound by 60 lb (27 kg) of chains before being padlocked in a metal cage and lowered into a transparent tank of water in Hollywood, California.

AMAZONIAN MAN

Dodging pirates, piranhas, whirlpools, sharks, and crocodiles, Martin Strel swam the mighty Amazon River in just 66 days.

On April 7, 2007, Martin, a 53-year-old from Slovenia, completed his colossal 3,274-mi (5,268-km) swim. From the Amazon's near-source in dense jungle around Atalaya in Peru across the vast width of Brazil to Bélem on the Atlantic coast, he swam a jaw-dropping average 50 mi (80 km), 10 hours a day, emerging from the water on the final afternoon exhausted and delirious, with blood pressure at near heart attack levels. He staggered to the ambulance still wearing the wet suit that had protected him from the snakes, spiders, and carnivorous fish that had chewed at his body during his remarkable adventure.

Throughout the mammoth journey, support crews in a boat beside him had tipped vast bucketloads of pig and chicken blood into the water in an attempt to lure the predators away. To work, the blood had to be old and the stench was revolting. The theory wasn't always successful—Martin was once pulled from the water yelling in agony, as a piranha gnawed into his leg. Other obstacles were women wielding machetes, murderous drug smugglers, and almost constant diarrhea (which had to be released into the said wetsuit and attracted more pests, including parasitic fish). But Strel was happy to add the Amazon to his list of conquests, and even happier to be on dry land!

Martin wore a pillowcase mask to help protect against sunburn.

Martin's incredible journey was the equivalent of swimming some 105,500 lengths of a 50-m (165-ft) pool.

Martin starts his swim weighing 253 lb (115 kg).

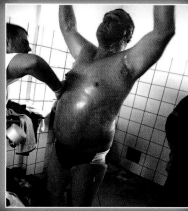

Grease is liberally applied at the beginning of the swim.

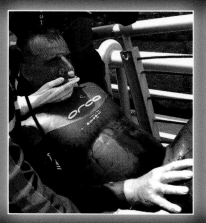

Martin receives extra oxygen at the end of a particularly hard day's swim.

Many of the perils faced by Martin were hidden in the murky water.

River Racer

Martin Strel taught himself to swim when he was six years old. Since then he's set the pace for distance swimming.

● **Danube River, June 25–August 23, 2000** First person to swim the river from source to estuary—1,867 mi (3,004 km)—passing through ten European countries in 58 days.

● **Danube River, July 2001** First to swim 313 mi (504 km) non-stop in 84 hours 10 minutes, the furthest distance ever swum without rest.

● **Mississippi River, July 4–September 9, 2002** Swam the whole length of the river—2,360 mi (3,797 km)—in 68 days, breaking his own previous record.

● **Paraná River, Argentina, November 15–December 8, 2003** Swam from the Iguazu Falls to the center of Buenos Aires (1,200 mi/1,930 km).

● **Yangtze River, June 10–July 30, 2004** Beat his achievements along the Mississippi by swimming 2,488 mi (4,003 km) of the longest Chinese river in 50 days.

Ripley's ask

How do you prepare for a swim? I train two times a day for three to five hours, in the pool or in the sea or lakes. I do this at least 400 times. I also do cross-country skiing, hiking, and gymnastics. During the swim, I eat lots of soup, pasta, and carbohydrates, and drink at least 10 liters of fluid a day—water, one cup of beer, and maybe a bottle of wine!

Why was the Amazon the most difficult river you have swum yet? The Amazon was recently confirmed as the longest river in the world, longer than the Nile. It is very special. Every hour of every day, there was one question: how to stay alive, just for that day. The water is muddy and you can't see anything, none of the dangers.

How did you stay alive? In my team, on a boat alongside me, I had two armed guards with Kalashnikovs [assault rifles] in case the pirates attacked. And they had buckets of blood and flesh ready to throw in the water to distract the piranhas. They had to be ready in seconds. If they had fallen asleep I would have died.

And what kept you going mentally? I knew I had to swim around 12 hours a day and cover 50 miles—it didn't matter if I was tired or sick. So I would talk to myself. I would go into a kind of trance, and sometimes even hallucinate. I had to be stronger than the Amazon.

What will you do next? I need half a year to recover—I will swim just 45 minutes a day. But then comes the next challenge. I won't swim the Nile—it's just a creek compared to the Amazon—but maybe a lake or sea.

Martin says that he swims "for peace, friendship, and clean water," and "to raise awareness of global warming."

Not all of the creatures that Martin encountered were bad for his health!

Exhausted but triumphant, and 36 lb (16 kg) lighter, at the end of the swim.

Finish

Start: Atalaya
February 1, 2007

PERU

Finish: Bélem
April 7, 2007

BRAZIL

🐂 bull shark
🔪 parasitic fish
🐟 piranha
🌀 whirlpool
☠ pirates
📱 smugglers

Enter the Vault

ANTONIO

Inflates a balloon with his ears

EXTRAORDINARY EARS

Cuban Antonio Galindo performed with the Ringling Circus in 1931—his specialty was using his ears to blow out candles and inflate balloons.

SUPERBABY

In 1950, strong and supple baby Philip Dellagrotti of Berwick, Pennsylvania, could swing impressively on his father's hands and hold himself out horizontally!

◀ MUSICAL ▶ MAYHEM

F.G. Holt of Nashville, Arkansas, used to demonstrate his ability to control every facial muscle by attaching bells to his eyebrows and playing some well-known tunes. And H.C. Harris, of Jackson, Mississippi, could play the harmonica and whistle at the same time!

◄ TOUGH TEETH

Joe Ponder of Love Valley, North Carolina, was a well-known strongman who performed lifts using his teeth. Here he is seen lifting a 500-lb (230-kg) mule with his champion choppers.

YOUNG AT HEART

In 1934, A.T. Brown of Grand Junction, Colorado, could slide head-first down 40-ft (12-m) telegraph poles at the grand old age of 80!

PICK-UP KING

In the 1930s, Julius Schuster of Jeannette, Pennsylvania, could pick up ten billiard balls in one hand, from a flat surface and without the aid of his other hand.

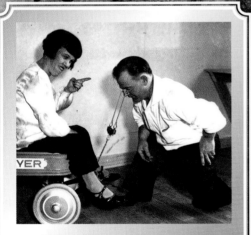

THE EYES HAVE IT

Performing at Ripley's Chicago Odditorium in 1933, Harry McGregor of Philadelphia, Pennsylvania, could pull his wife Lillian around in a wagon—a load of 150 lb (68 kg)—with his eyelids!

PLAYING PIGGYBACK

Jack Trimbledon (bottom) led a novelty orchestra in the 1930s and 1940s. Here, two bandmates play while riding piggyback on Jack's back.

CAN DO!
In June 2007, three men from Queensland, Australia, sailed nearly 50 mi (80 km) down the Brisbane River in a boat made from beer cans.

TIRE CRAFT
Cheng Yanhua traveled more than 1,500 mi (2,400 km) down China's Yangtze River in 2007—on a tire inner tube. Using two small bamboo paddles, and with a basin in the tire for his feet, he took 43 days to get from his home in Jinzhou City to Shanghai.

BIKING MARATHON
In a three-month journey in 2007, British actor Ewan McGregor and his friend Charley Boorman rode their motorcycles 15,000 mi (24,000 km) from the most northerly point of Scotland to the southern tip of South Africa. Three years earlier, they rode their bikes from London, England, to New York via central Europe and Asia—20,000 mi (32,000 km).

SLOW ROUTE
Choosing not to fly for environmental reasons, Barbara Haddrill spent six months traveling by bus, train, and cargo ship on a 9,770-mi (15,725-km) journey from Powys, Wales, to attend her best friend's wedding in Brisbane, Australia.

MARATHON SWIM
In September 2007, Firas al Mualla swam 68 mi (110 km) nonstop across the Mediterranean Sea in 42 hours from Cyprus to his native Syria.

ROUND THE WORLD

Jamaican-born Barrington Irving of Miami, Florida, flew solo around the world in 2007—at just 23 years of age. His epic flight in a single-engine plane took three months, and on the way he encountered snowstorms, sandstorms, thunderstorms, monsoons, 100-mph (160-km/h) winds, and freezing fog. He named his plane "Inspiration" because, he said, "that's what I wanted my historic venture to be for young people."

BUMPY RIDE
Two British students traveled a distance of 9,500-mi (15,300-km) through 14 countries, three mountain ranges, and two deserts—in a car designed 60 years ago. George Vlasto and Max Benitz drove from the University of Calcutta, India, to London, England, in an Ambassador car that was held together by two rolls of duct tape.

HIGH NOTES
Six British and U.S. musicians played a rock concert at a height of 18,540 ft (5,650 m) on Mount Everest in October 2007. The six were Mike Peters of The Alarm, Slim Jim Phantom of the Stray Cats, Cy Curnin and Jamie West-Oram of the Fixx, and Glenn Tilbrook and Nick Harper of Squeeze.

UNICYCLE TEAM
A dozen cyclists rode 560 mi (900 km) across New Zealand's South Island in 15 days in 2007—on unicycles.

DESERT RUN
Charlie Engle (United States), Ray Zahab (Canada), and Kevin Lin (Taiwan) ran the equivalent of two marathons a day for 111 days to cross the entire 4,000-mi (6,440-km) Sahara Desert on foot in 2007. They ran through six countries—Senegal, Mauritania, Mali, Niger, Libya, and Egypt—and had to cope with temperatures over 100°F (38°C) by day, but sometimes below freezing at night.

HISTORICAL VOYAGE
Taking the same route as his ancestor Christopher Columbus had 508 years earlier, Scottish stockbroker Leven Brown rowed single-handed across the Atlantic from Cadiz, Spain, to the port of Scarborough in Trinidad and Tobago. Rowing up to 18 hours each day, Brown completed the 4,278-mi (6,885-km) voyage in five months. Apart from storms, his biggest problem came from whales that wanted to use his 23-ft (7-m) boat as a scratching post!

WEARY LEGS
In 2007, Greg Kolodziejzyk of Calgary, Alberta, Canada, traveled 107 mi (172 km) by pedal boat in 24 hours around the city's Glenmore Reservoir.

"Two days into the nine-month journey, 350 mi (560 km) from civilization, on the North Slope Brooks Mountain Range, Alaska."

"No water, 6 mi (9.5 km) to next water source, 100°F (38°C) heat."

AMERICAN ODYSSEY

Starting in May 2007, Quinn Baumberger of Stevens Point, Wisconsin, cycled for nine months and traveled more than 19,000 mi (30,600 km) the length of the Americas from Deadhorse, Alaska, to Ushuaia, Argentina. Along the way, he fixed 50 flat tires, was robbed twice, and sprained his ankle in Nicaragua, which put him out of action for two weeks. He replaced his old, worn shirts with those he found on the road.

TRACTOR TREK

Tractor fan Wolfgang Mueller drove his 44-year-old tractor 700 mi (1,130 km) from Stuttgart, Germany, to Coventry, England, in 2007. He towed a caravan through Luxembourg and France, boarded a ferry at Calais, and drove the tractor sedately through English country lanes. He wanted to visit the place where his beloved Massey Ferguson MF35 had been built—only to find that the factory had been demolished.

CHICKEN WING HUNT

In August 2007, Matt Reynolds led a team of fellow food enthusiasts on a 2,627-mi (4,230-km) trek through New York State in search of the best chicken wings. The Great Chicken Wing Hunt began in Manhattan and ended in Buffalo at the National Wing Festival. Reynolds and his team eventually crowned chef Columbus Grady, of Abigail's Restaurant in Seneca Falls, maker of the best wings in the whole of New York state.

ICY SWIM

In 2004, Lynne Cox of Southern California, completed a 25-minute, 1.2-mi (1.9-km) swim through the polar ice water along the Antarctic shoreline, in water temperatures that would have given most people hypothermia in just five minutes.

DOUBLE FIRST

In July 2006, 15-year-old Jenna Lambert from Kingston, Ontario, Canada, became the first disabled person to swim across Lake Ontario. Jenna has cerebral palsy, and could use only her upper body—not her legs—to swim, but despite strong winds and waves, she completed the 21-mi (34-km) swim in 32 hours. Then, a year later, her 14-year-old sister Natalie became the youngest person to swim the lake when she made a 32½-mi (52-km) crossing from Sackets Harbor, New York, to Kingston in under 24 hours.

SIMPLY BREATHTAKING

In August 2007, German diver Tom Sietas managed to hold his breath underwater for 15 minutes 2 seconds—without surfacing once. He breathed in oxygen from a tank for 20 minutes beforehand to help prepare his body for the feat.

BALLPARK TOUR

Brothers Brigham and Todd Shearon from Windsor, Ontario, Canada, visited all 30 major-league baseball stadiums in 28 days in 2007—a journey of 14,500 mi (23,000 km).

BIKE TRAVELS

Gregory Frazier of Fort Smith, Montana, has ridden around the world on a motorcycle five times—four solo and the fifth, in 2005, with a 63-year-old grandmother of six on the back of the bike. He has traveled more than one million miles (1.6 million km), riding from Alaska to Tierra del Fuego, and Norway to the tip of South Africa. In the course of his adventures, he has been imprisoned, bitten by snakes, run over by bulls, had his bike stolen, and been held up at gunpoint by a Mexican bandit.

Eurasian Trek

In September 2007, Australian Tim Cope completed a 3½-year, 6,200-mi (10,000-km), solo trek across some of the harshest terrain on the planet, from Mongolia to Hungary, following in the footsteps of the 13th-century Mongolian warlord Genghis Khan.

En route he endured temperatures ranging from –54ºF (–52ºC) to 130ºF (54ºC), had his horses and his dog stolen, and survived a night surrounded by howling wolves hungry for their next meal.

The inspiration for this epic journey was a desire to understand what life is like for the nomadic people who populate the steppes of Asia and Central Europe. When Tim from Gippsland, Victoria, set off in June 2004, he expected his journey to take 18 months,

but unforeseen delays, including extreme weather, long border hold-ups, and the death of his father, meant that Tim's epic journey took much longer.

Throughout the trek, Tim traveled with three horses—one to carry him and two to carry food and supplies—even though at the start he could barely ride a horse. He needed 13 horses in total to complete his marathon adventure, and in Kazakhstan he also used a camel to combat the intense heat. At other times he had to ride headlong into fierce blizzards, guided only by a compass.

The animals were his lifeline, so he was devastated when just five days into his travels, two of his horses were stolen in the dead of night. With the help of a Mongolian herdsman, they were returned the next day and Tim quickly came to appreciate the value of striking up friendships on the

steppes. Around 160 families welcomed the stranger into their homes. "They were the real heroes of my journey," he said.

In Kazakhstan, Tim kept predatory wolves at bay by throwing firecrackers—a tip he picked up from the local people. Describing his fear of these animals, he said: "When you hear that howl alone at night in the forest, it's one of the most frightening sounds you'll ever hear."

On eventually reaching his destination, the Hungarian town of Opusztaszer on the river Danube, he admitted: "Sometimes I didn't think I would ever arrive." However, his joy at achieving his goal was tempered by having to let the animals go. "I'm feeling a bit panicky," he said, "because I can't imagine saying goodbye to the horses. A lot has happened in my life during this journey."

Tim with Tigon, which means "hawk" in Kazakh, in the Carpathian Mountains.

Pausing in the Harhiraa Mountains of western Mongolia in September 2004.

Tim Cope's faithful companion on his travels was Tigon, a black Kazakh hunting dog given to him by villagers in Kazakhstan. After Tigon was snatched by rustlers, a villager found the dog nearly frozen to death, locked inside an ice-filled mine shaft. He nursed Tigon back to health by putting him in a hot sauna and feeding him a diet of raw eggs and vodka. Nevertheless, it was three weeks before Tigon was fit enough to resume the journey.

Tim and his leading horse, Taskonir, taking a dip in the Black Sea in the Ukraine.

In Kazakhstan with his three horses, Tim heads into his first winter of the trip.

Ripley's ask

How did you plan for the journey? The majority of the planning was done by reading and getting help from the Long Riders' Guild, who are a group of experienced equestrian explorers who thought my journey was historically important. I knew that I would need at least three horses—one for equipment, one for grain, and one for myself. Looking after them was also important, so I met with an equine vet who was always ready to help me, even via satellite phone when I was in the saddle. I also trained in Australia with some packhorse tour leaders.

What was the hardest part of the journey? There were many hard parts. The winter of 2004–05 when I was stuck in winter storms on the betpak dala ("starving steppe") was particularly bad. My horse developed an abscess, my tent ripped, my sleeping bag froze, and the only place we found for shelter was with some alcoholics in a gold-mining village, who served up boiled street pigeon for Christmas lunch. I was stuck there for almost three months. The temperature that year in Kazakhstan dropped as low as –54°F (–52°C).

What inspired you to carry on? Whenever it was really hard, I only had to think about the nomads. They had to deal with these problems and hardships all their lives. I was inspired by their strength to carry on.

What kind of things did you eat? I drank fermented mares' milk daily, and carried dried mutton with me called "borts." This dried meat is so compact that Mongolians say you can carry a whole sheep in your pocket! The first sight of a camel, horse, or lamb's head on the table was a bit of a shock!

What kind of places did you sleep in? I mostly slept in my own tent, family yurt tents, or village homes that ranged from underground mud huts to large mudbrick and wooden homes.

What was the most vital piece of equipment you took with you? I would have to say my pen and diary! I love writing and getting all my thoughts, feelings, and impressions down.

POLAR TREK

Explorer Hannah McKeand from Berkshire, England, completed a solo, unsupported 690-mi (1,110-km) trek across Antarctica to the South Pole in less than 40 days in 2006. On skis and dragging a 220-lb (100-kg) sled, she faced temperatures lower than −40°F (−40°C) and winds of more than 70 mph (112 km/h).

GLOBE RUNNER

A man dubbed the British "Forrest Gump" ran around the world over a period of 5 years 8 months. Robert Garside from the town of Stockport in Cheshire, England, ran more than 35,000 mi (56,000 km) and crossed through 30 countries between 1997 and 2003. On the way he was jailed in China, threatened at gunpoint in Panama, and met his future wife in Venezuela.

PARTY GIRL

Evelyn Warburton of Berwick, Pennsylvania, rode to her 100th birthday party in September 2007 in a motorcycle sidecar—wearing a black leather jacket and a cool pair of sunglasses.

BLADE RUNNER

Even though his legs were amputated below the knee when he was 11 months old, South African sprinter Oscar Pistorius races against—and beats—able-bodied athletes. Pistorius can run 400 meters in 46.34 seconds—just three seconds outside Michael Johnson's world record—on carbon-fiber artificial legs that have earned him the nickname of Blade Runner.

VETERAN RUNNER

Although he never ran a full mile until he was nearly 50, George Etzweiler of State College, Pennsylvania, has been making up for lost time ever since. In June 2007, the active 87-year-old completed the Mount Washington Road Race in New Hampshire—a 7.6-mi (12.2-km) course featuring an uphill climb with a daunting 11.5 percent incline.

VETERAN JUMPER

In August 2007, an 83-year-old New York skydiver made his 100th jump from an airplane. A veteran of World War II, Leo Dean took up skydiving after he was widowed in 1998. He's now aiming for 200 jumps.

PADDLE POWER

Margo Pellegrino of Medford Lakes, New Jersey, paddled her kayak some 2,000 mi (3,220 km) along the east coast of the United States in 2007 from Miami, Florida, to Camden, Maine, covering an average of 40 mi (65 km) a day.

ECHO SKILL

Daniel Kish of Long Beach, California, is completely blind but can ride a bike using echolocation, just like a bat or a dolphin, to "see" objects with sound.

VERSATILE COOK

Krishnaveni Mudliar, a housewife from Bhopal, India, can cook nearly 65,000 different recipes. She can prepare recipes from every state in India as well as Italian, Chinese, and Burmese dishes.

AUTOGRAPH FRENZY

To promote his latest album "West Side," Singaporean pop singer J.J. Lin signed his autograph on 3,052 copies of the album's CD in 2½ hours in Tianjin, China, in July 2007.

• • • KAYAK CROSSING • • •

Two Australian adventurers completed a historic crossing of the Tasman Sea by kayak—less than one year after another Australian, Andrew McAuley, died while attempting the same feat. James Castrission and Justin Jones, both from Sydney, finished the arduous 2,050-mi (3,300-km) journey—known locally as "crossing the ditch"—from Forster, New South Wales, to Ngamotu Beach on New Zealand's North Island in 62 days. They arrived in early January 2008—20 days later than anticipated after strong winds and stormy seas left them floundering in circles halfway through the trip and nearly forced them to turn back. They also had to fend off the unwelcome attention of sharks.

Their voyage had taken four years' intense preparation, including sleep deprivation and isolation training. Afterward, Castrission acknowledged the value of having a companion to lean on. "Some nights when we were out there," he said, "we had each other to hold through the difficult moments."

Although the kayak was designed to combat 40-ft (12-m) waves, crossing the Tasman Sea proved a daunting prospect and sometimes Jones and Castrission had to paddle in shifts for 18 hours a day.

SUMMIT TALKS

A British climber made a cell-phone call from the top of Mount Everest in 2007. Rod Baber was able to make two calls from the 29,029-ft (8,848-m) mountain after China set up a new mobile base station. Even making a short call at such an altitude was hazardous for Baber, as talking into the handset meant removing his oxygen mask.

TWO-DAY MATCH

Brian Jahrsdoerfer and Michel Lavoie played fellow Americans Peter Okpokpo and Warner Tse in a doubles tennis match that lasted 48 hours 15 minutes at Westside Tennis Club, Houston, Texas, in April 2006.

SUPER COACH

Robert Hughes of Fort Worth, Texas, retired in 2005 with 1,333 wins to his name—more than any other high-school basketball coach in U.S history.

WINNING STREAK

The boys' football team at De La Salle High School, Concord, California, had a 12-season, 151-game winning streak from 1992 to 2004.

PUSH-UPS

Roy Berger of Ottawa, Ontario, Canada, completed more than 1,000 fist push-ups in just under 17 minutes in May 2007. He did not even break a sweat until he hit 400.

SNOWMOBILE JUMP

Ross Mercer of Whitehorse, Yukon, Canada, jumped his snowmobile 263½ ft (80.3 m) high at Steamboat Springs, Colorado, in March 2007.

CABLE CAR

In 2007, Liu Suozhu of Korla City, China, drove his pickup truck for 15 minutes along 200 yd (180 m) of parallel steel cables that were stretched more than 60 ft (18 m) in the air between two hills.

HIGH RIDERS

In April 2007, two Chilean men drove a car to an altitude of 21,942 ft (6,688 m). After two failed attempts to reach extreme altitudes, driver Gonzalo Bravo and his spotter Eduardo Canales piloted their modified 1986 Suzuki Samurai to the highest slopes of the Ojos del Salado volcano in Chile's Atacama Desert.

DANCING FOOL

The U.K.'s official state jester, as named by the national charity English Heritage, Peterkin the Fool—alias Peet Cooper—danced a jig for 28 days on a 100-mi (160-km) journey from Bristol to Northampton, England, in July 2006. He was commemorating the 100-mi jig-journey made in 1599 by Will Kemp, a Shakespearean court jester.

SENIOR HERDSMAN

Li Xicai still works as a herdsman in the mountainous Kuangshi village of China, at the age of 107. He has been herding animals all his life and still herds bulls in the mountains every day.

FLOAT ON

Keeping his hands behind his head and his toes above the surface at all times, Andrzej Szopinski-Wisla of Poland floated on water for more than two hours in 2006.

CLUB JUGGLER

Iryna Bilenka of the Ukraine can juggle three clubs for nearly two minutes—while wearing a blindfold!

When conditions were favorable, the intrepid adventurers were able to paddle at speeds of up to 6 mph (10 km/h).

Justin keeping the website account of their epic journey up to date in the kayak's sleeping quarters.

TUXEDO TRAVELERS

Two men completed a five-month, 6,214-mi (10,000-km) trek from Hong Kong to London—dressed the entire way in tuxedos.

Briton Heath Buck and American Doug Campbell dreamed up their bizarre charity adventure in a Hong Kong bar in 2005 despite having known each other for only a few days. Before setting off on April Fool's Day 2007, the pair—who promoted themselves as "two fools, one adventure, no idea"—trashed their ordinary clothes and donned the tuxedos, which had been specially made for them in Bangkok, Thailand, from extra-resilient fabric and fitted with hidden pockets for valuables.

Apart from sleeping and showering, they wore their dinner dress every step of the way on a journey that took them through remote regions of China, Vietnam, Tibet, Nepal, India, Pakistan, and Kyrgyzstan—among other places.

In Vietnam, they plowed rice paddies, weeded corn crops, and built a wall—still wearing their black suits and bow ties. "It was quite a surreal experience," admitted Campbell. "At the end we brought a few of the local tribal women to tears when we donated fertilizer for the year's crop. In return they made us honorary tribe members."

The pair also went wrestling in India and had to deal with temperatures of over 120°F (50°C), but the tuxedos survived to the finish. Not surprisingly, the two men got some odd looks along the way. "Everyone asked if they could take a picture of us," said Buck. "They often asked us if we were getting married!"

Doug and Heath modeling their special tuxedos made at a tailor in Bangkok, Thailand.

Posing with people dressed in traditional costume in Yangshuo, China.

Doug and a member of the Dao Hill Tribe in Vietnam.

The guys stayed with the Dao Hill Tribe and helped them with buffalo plowing.

Heath gives a rickshaw rider a much needed break in Kathmandu.

Doug with a Tibetan man while in Shangri La in China's Yunnan Province.

The two men were made honorary members of the tribe on their departure.

Heath hosted an English tea party at Everest Base camp.

Heath jumping the Taj Mahal in India.

While staying in freezing conditions at an altitude of 9,800 ft (3,000 m) in Kyrgyzstan, Heath and Doug's tuxedos provided much-needed warmth.

Wearing Kyrgyzstani robes gave their tuxedos a local feel in Kyrgyzstan.

Approaching England's famous white cliffs of Dover at the end of their journey.

Ripley's ask

How did you meet? DOUG: We met randomly in Hong Kong at a street party. HEATH: We exchanged e-mails after making a pact to save the world! Doug was committed to not being outdone by me, whatever my imagination could come up with.

Why decide to travel in tuxedos? DOUG: Heath came up with the tuxedo idea. I said I'd join only if we could add a charitable angle—so we weren't just being idiots, but idiots on a quest! And so the planning began...

Was there a point at which you really wished you weren't wearing tuxedos? DOUG: India, India, India!! It was so hot and also the early part of the monsoon season so very humid and wet. I also had giardia [a parasite in the small intestine] and was pretty upset about the whole situation. We were close to calling the trip off, but settled our differences and Heath's classic English resolve pulled us through!

How did people react to you? DOUG: As far as the tuxedos went—people thought we were going to a marriage, or that we were Western businessmen, professional snooker players, religious missionaries, jazz musicians, magicians, or otherwise just complete nut-jobs!

What was your biggest achievement during the tuxedo challenge? DOUG: Besides successfully completing the mission (a feat many thought we would fail at), I believe we showed our audience that the world is a friendly place. People were often surprised that we survived, but I usually joke that I've felt more scared in downtown L.A. than anywhere along our route! HEATH: I think my biggest achievement was working with T.B. patients at one charity mission, where we were actively joining in with a charity's dedication to save people's lives.

What was the strangest thing you did on your journey wearing a tuxedo?! DOUG: Laughing Therapy in India had to be up there with one of the funniest moments. We found a man in Rishikesh who led us, along with a few other backpackers, into a hilarious session of deep belly laughing exercises! This was meant to calm you and relieve you of external stresses. We certainly had fun so I guess it worked! HEATH: Horseback riding over the mountains in Kyrgyzstan. We added a Kyrgyz robe to our tuxedos, and with robes flowing in the wind, we precariously picked our way through a mountain pass, where when you looked down you realized that one slip and you'd be falling into oblivion.

Do you have any plans for another tuxedo journey? HEATH: We intend to keep on arranging random groups of tuxedo-clad people to turn up and perform acts of charity across the globe! I am also planning another trip, but this time it will be along a superhero theme to help save the world!

Phoebe Syms from London, England, has collected nearly 4,000 erasers. Her obsession began at just two years of age, when she was attracted by the smell and feel of them. Fourteen years later, her collection is still going strong.

STAGE FAN

Andrea Schecter of Oceanside, New York, has a collection of approximately 2,300 playbills from the stage shows that she has seen, from New York to London.

LIGHTERS GALORE

Ted Ballard of Guthrie, Oklahoma, started collecting cigarette lighters when he was six years old and at the last count had a collection of more than 20,000.

BEER CANS

Australia's John Loveday has a collection of more than 6,000 beer cans from 78 countries—and he doesn't even drink! He has been collecting beer-related memorabilia for more than 15 years and also has 1,500 beer glasses, 900 beer bottles, plus assorted beer-themed coasters, matchboxes, key rings, bottle tops, and mirrors.

TIE PINS

Since 1977, Kevin Godden of Kent, England, has been collecting tie pins—and he now has more than 1,300 of them.

UNIQUE ATTRACTION

In the basement of his home at Onset, Massachusetts, Dick Porter has more than 5,000 thermometers—the result of some 25 years of collecting. He calls it the world's largest and only thermometer museum.

GREEN LIGHT

A 14-year-old boy from Merseyside, England, has been given the green light to collect traffic signals. Simon Patterson already has six sets of lights, more than 30 beacons, and hundreds of photographs of traffic lights from around the world sent to him by friends on holiday. He has built up his collection, which also includes numerous road signs, by writing to councils or buying old sets on eBay at about $50 each.

CONE ZONE

David Morgan's life is dedicated to traffic cones. Not only does he work for the world's largest producer of cones, but he has a collection of 500 of them at his home in Oxfordshire, England. He has been collecting them for more than 20 years, usually from roadworks, where he swaps a sought-after cone for a brand new one. Among his prized possessions are a Malaysian cone, found washed up on a beach in the Isles of Scilly off the southwest coast of the U.K., and a rare 1980 cone, which he picked up at an airport in Corsica while on his honeymoon.

POINT MADE

John Little never forgot being told off at school for not having a pencil sharpener, so now he has more than 1,500. John, from County Durham, England, has been collecting sharpeners for 20 years and has examples from all over the world in such diverse shapes as a kiwi, a banana, a red letter box, an apple, a wooden clog, and a shark.

CALL CENTER

The exterior of a small electronics store in Tokyo, Japan, is decorated with 6,000 used cell phones. The shop's owner, Masanao Watanabe, has been collecting them since 1994 and decided on the unusual display when he ran out of storage space inside. Now visitors come from all over the city to study the walls and see if they can find models they have owned.

PERFECT MATCH

Joe DeGennaro of New York City, has a collection of more than 100,000 matchcovers and matchboxes. He is a leading light of the Rathkamp Matchcover Society—named after its founder and avid matchbox collector Henry Rathkamp—which boasts more than 1,000 members across North America.

LIQUOR HAUL

Leonard White, a businessman from Vancouver, British Columbia, Canada, spent decades collecting more than 8,000 unopened miniature liquor bottles. Their shapes range from Elvis Presley to airplanes to animals.

SPACE DEBRIS

Jim Bernath of Burnaby, British Columbia, Canada, collects debris from old satellites and crashed comets. His collection includes old loaves of bread from the Russian space station *Mir* and pieces of satellites belonging to countries as far afield as Canada, Hungary, Italy, and Spain.

COOKIE-JAR MONSTER

Starting in 1975, Lucille Bromberek of Lemont, Illinois, collected cookie jars and eventually amassed more than 2,000.

BAG LADY

Carol Vaughan from Birmingham, England, has collected more than 8,000 carrier bags in all shapes and sizes. The 64-year-old, who hates throwing things away, also has a house full of 52 other collections, including 2,500 bars of soap, 500 tins, and 400 mugs.

HAMMER HOME

Germany's George Peters has been fascinated by hammers for 30 years and now has over 3,500 in his collection. His hammers come from all over the world and range in weight from a tiny 0.0006 oz (0.017 g) to a hefty 155 lb (70 kg).

FISHY BUSINESS

Bob Toelle of British Columbia, Canada, collects fish posters of the world. He has more than 700 fish posters displayed on his website, and his most recent additions include Pacific Northwest Spawning Salmon and Threatened Freshwater Fish of Croatia.

RARE CORKSCREWS

Nicholas Hunt of Sydney, New South Wales, Australia, has been collecting corkscrews from around the world for over a decade and now has more than 1,000. One of the oldest dates back to 1838.

Perfect Perspective

As a child, Stephen Wiltshire was mute and did not relate to other people. Diagnosed as autistic, he had uncontrolled tantrums, lived entirely in his own world, and did not learn to speak fully until he was nine. Yet he has an incredible talent for drawing and can produce remarkably accurate and detailed pictures entirely from memory.

Just by looking once at a building, Stephen can reproduce its likeness faithfully on paper. As a 12-year-old, he drew from memory a brilliant sketch of London's St. Pancras station, which he had visited for the first time only briefly a few hours earlier. He even drew the station clock hands at 11:20, the precise time at which he had viewed them.

In 2001, after flying in a helicopter over London, he drew in three hours an aerial illustration of a 4-sq-mi (10-sq-km) area of the city, featuring 12 major landmarks and 200 other buildings, all in perfect perspective and scale. In 2005, following a short helicopter ride over Tokyo, he drew a stunningly detailed panoramic view of the city on a 33-ft-long (10-m) canvas. Since then he has drawn Rome, Hong Kong, and Frankfurt on giant canvases.

Stephen can also draw from imagination. When he was eight he was shown photographs of earthquakes in a book and promptly drew fantastic cityscapes showing the aftermath of an earthquake. His artwork is now so valued that he has his own permanent gallery in London.

The Royal Albert Hall, London

Stephen wiltshire

Downtown Manhattan, New York City

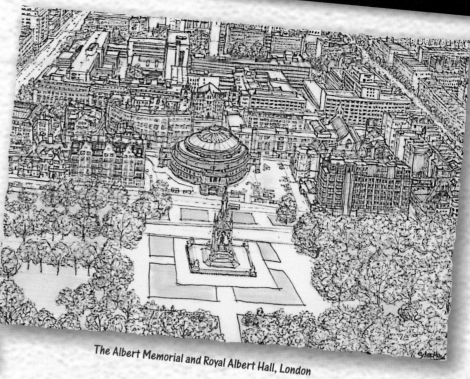

The Albert Memorial and Royal Albert Hall, London

UNUSUAL GENIUS

● Diagnosed with mental illness at birth, Kim Peek from Salt Lake City, Utah, reads up to eight books a day. He reads at a phenomenal rate, scanning the left page with his left eye and the right page with his right eye, and retaining around 98 per cent of the information. He can read in ten seconds a page that would take most adults three minutes.

● Tony DeBlois from Randolph, Massachusetts, was born blind but began to play the piano at the age of two. He now plays 20 musical instruments and can play more than 8,000 songs from memory.

● David Kidd can barely perform simple arithmetic, yet if he hears a random date—past, present, or future—he can immediately pinpoint on which day of the week it occurred or will occur.

● Derek Paravicini from Surrey, England, is blind and has a severe learning disability, but he can play back a piece of music after hearing it just once.

● England's Daniel Tammet can perform complex mathematical calculations at amazing speeds—he can figure out cube roots quicker than a calculator and recall pi to 22,514 decimal places. Yet because of his autism, he can't tell left from right.

● Despite being born blind with brain damage and never having had a piano lesson in his life, Leslie Lemke from Milwaukee, Wisconsin, played Tchaikovsky's Piano Concerto No. 1 after hearing it for the first time on TV.

The Chrysler Building, New York City

HOT WHEELS

Michael Zarnock of Deerfield, New York, has 8,128 different Hot Wheels cars—part of his collection of more than 25,000 model cars. Many of them are on display at the Children's Museum in Utica, New York, where they occupy seven glass cabinets, each 12 ft (3.6 m) in length. He says: "To this day, every birthday or holiday, everyone knows what to get me."

My Fascination with Hot Wheels!

"I started collecting Hot Wheels cars when they were first released in 1968. I think the first car I bought was the Silhouette. I remembered seeing it on an episode of 'Mission Impossible' and fell in love with that car.

My mother still reminds me of the Christmas that I bought everyone in the family Hot Wheels for Christmas gifts. I knew they wouldn't want them and they would give them to me. Not a bad idea for a ten-year-old. Too bad it didn't work. I had to go out and buy everybody new gifts.

I'm also a package collector. I like the different styles of the packages from the many eras of Hot Wheels. Like I've always said, it's all about the memories for me. Hot Wheels relax me and bring me back to the easygoing childhood I once knew. I keep everything in its original package. My saying is: "Preserve the toy, preserve the boy." There isn't a day that goes by that I don't shop or look for something to add to my collection—either looking in any store that I drive by or on the Internet at the auction sites. Sadly, it's gotten to the point that there aren't too many items that I don't already have, but I always keep checking! You never know, I may get surprised and find something that I didn't know existed.

I have been obsessed with Hot Wheels cars and accessories for the past 40 years, and I look forward to continuing to collect them for the next 40 years!"

MURDER MUSEUM

As well as sculptures of Charles Manson and notorious cannibals, the Serial Killer Museum in Florence, Italy, recounts the crimes of American murderers John Wayne Gacy and Ted Bundy. It also houses mock-ups of a gas chamber and an electric chair.

WALLPAPER MUSEUM

In France there is a museum devoted to wallpaper. Le Musée du Papier Peint at Rixheim has a history of wallpaper along with demonstrations of its manufacture.

MAGICAL MARBLES

As well as chronicling the history of marbles, the Marble Museum at Yreka, California, houses beautiful, hand-painted china marbles, as well as a collection of paintings about marbles.

DISCARDED OBJECTS

Artist Rebecca Wolfram of Chicago, Illinois, has set up a Museum of Objects Left on the Sidewalk—a collection of items abandoned in the street, including used fireworks, broken dolls, sweat shirts, gloves, pots and pans, and a wire coat-hanger molded into the shape of a shark.

CURIOSITY CABINET

Keswick Museum in Cumbria, England, is home to a "Cabinet of Curiosities," including a 14-ft-long (4-m), 1.5-ton xylophone made of slate, a 665-year-old cat, the Emperor Napoleon's teacup, poet Robert Southey's clogs, a spoon made from the leg bone of a sheep, and a man trap.

DRAIN TILES

Housed in the 1822 home of John Johnston, a pioneer in tile drainage technology, the Mike Weaver Drain Tile Museum at Geneva, New York, boasts a collection of more than 500 drain tiles dating from 500 BC to the modern plastic version. Marion "Mike" Weaver worked in drainage for 20 years and started his collection in 1950.

TWISTED LOGIC

In Dannebrog, Nebraska, there is a museum dedicated to liars. Nothing is as it seems at the Liar's Hall of Fame, where exhibits include a box of golf balls the size of hailstones!

SEWER MUSEUM

In Hamburg, Germany, there is a museum dedicated to objects found in the city's sewer system.

DAIRY DELIGHTS

America's Ice Cream and Dairy Museum at Medina, Ohio, has artifacts on the history of ice cream dating back to ancient Egypt. Among the most cherished exhibits is a 1905 "gaslight" soda fountain.

DRUM DREAM

Alan Buckley of Walsall, England, started collecting drum kits at the age of eight—and now he has 110 of them. The 72-year-old musician, known as "Sir Alan" after his friends bought him a "knighthood," has snares dating back to 1809 and numerous other drums from the 1920s and 1930s. His collection includes a drum from London's Windmill Theatre, famous for never closing during World War II.

TROLL COLLECTION
More than 400 trolls in different sizes and outfits are housed in a troll museum in New York City run by Jen Miller.

DEAD TICKS
The Smithsonian Institute Tick Museum in Statesboro, Georgia, has a collection of more than one million dead ticks.

SWEET SPOT
The Marzipan Museum in Keszthely, Hungary, has displays of sculpture—including dragons, shields, and miniature palaces—all made out of marzipan.

VINTAGE VODKA
In Moscow, Russia, there is a vodka museum containing 50,000 bottles of vodka, some as much as 200 years old.

NONPROFIT
The Ohio-based International Brick Collectors' Association forbids its 1,000-plus members to buy or sell bricks for money.

POPCORN MACHINES
The Wyandot Popcorn Museum at Marion, Ohio, boasts the largest collection of popcorn and peanut roasters in the world, with some items dating back to the 1890s. It has more than 50 antique popping machines, including one used by movie star Paul Newman to promote his own popcorn in Central Park, New York.

HUGE NICKEL
Among more than one million vintage pieces at the Wooden Nickel Historical Museum at San Antonio, Texas, is a wooden nickel measuring 13 ft 4 in (4 m) in diameter and weighing 2,500 lb (1,135 kg).

VOODOO EXPERIENCE
The New Orleans Historic Voodoo Museum brings together ancient and modern voodoo practices. It houses artifacts such as dolls and memorabilia relating to the 19th-century voodoo queen Marie Laveau.

ROLLER SKATING
There is a museum in Lincoln, Nebraska, that is dedicated to roller skating. The National Museum of Roller Skating has a large collection of historical roller skates and costumes.

PARASITE PARADISE
The Meguro Parasitological Museum in Tokyo, Japan, has a collection of more than 300 parasites, including a tapeworm 30 ft (9 m) long that was pulled out of a person's body.

BRAIN MUSEUM

A museum in Lima, Peru, houses almost three thousand diseased human brains. Unlike most brain collections around the world, it is open to the public. Exhibits include the brain of someone who died from the human variant of "mad cow" disease, the brains of people who died of trichinosis—the most common brain disease in Peru—which is caused by eating undercooked meat, and several human fetuses with neurological disorders.

Ken and Annie Burkitt of Niagara Falls, Ontario, Canada, used more than one million genuine Austrian Swarovski lead crystals to decorate a 2004 Mini Cooper car with images of 11 of the United States' most recognizable and enduring iconic emblems.

The mural-style design includes the Statue of Liberty, Mount Rushmore, the American flag, and the famous Hollywood sign. It took four artists six months to place each crystal individually on the "American Icon" by hand. The crystals are all the exact same size and are in 50 different shades of color to represent the 50 states of the United States. Ken Burkitt said: "We wanted to create something that would pay tribute to America in an eye-catching way. The car takes on a completely different look as the lighting changes throughout the day. The crystal design takes on a life of its own."

The sparkling car is completely functional and marked another milestone for the creative husband-and-wife team. They had previously covered a limousine in 23,000 gold coins and a double-decker London bus in 100,000 gold-plated British pennies.

THE DESIGN

Back: The White House

Roof: Bald Eagle and the U.S. flag

Left side: Hollywood Hills sign; Space Shuttle; Capitol Building and Washington Monument; New York City skyline featuring the Chrysler Building

Right side: The Alamo and Mount Rushmore

Front: The Statue of Liberty

Page numbers in *italics* refer
to illustrations

ACKNOWLEDGMENTS

COVER (t/r) Reinhold Kringel Münster/Germany; BACK COVER Antonia Bolingbroke-Kent and Jo Huxster www.tuktotheroad.com; 4 Kent Couch – www.couchballoons.com; 6–7 (dps) Pete Erickson/AP/PA Photos, (b/l, b/c, b/r, l) Ken Couch – www.couchballoons.com; 8 Steve Colligan; 9 Antonia Bolingbroke-Kent and Jo Huxster www.tuktotheroad.com, (b) Jon Ross; 10 (sp) Volker Hartmann/AFP/Getty Images, (b/l) Axel Schmidt/AFP/Getty Images, (b/r) Reinhold Kringel Münster/Germany; 11 (t/l, t/r) Reinhold Kringel Münster/Germany, (b) Oliver Krato/DPA/PA Photos; 12 Keith Sharples/Rex Features; 13 Gabriel Bouys/AFP/Getty Images; 14–15 www.amazonswim.com; 18 (l, r) Juan Rivera Just Film Media, LLC, (c) Jon Ross; 19 (t, t/r) Quinn Joseph Baumberger, (b) Dr. Gregory W. Frazier www.horizonsunlimited.com/gregfrazier; 20–21 www.timcopejourneys.com; 22–23 www.crossingtheditch.com.au; 24–25 Heath and Doug, The Tuxedo Travellers; 26 (t) Phoebe Syms, (b) Ben Cawthra/Rex Features; 27 (t) Simon Jones/Rex Features, (r) Masatoshi Okauchi/Rex Features; 28 (c, b/l) Gary Bishop/Rex Features, (b/r) Steve Geer/iStockphoto; 29 Gary Bishop/Rex Features; 30 Michael Zarnock www.MikeZarnock.com; 31 (t) Daniel Graves/Rex Features, (b) Reuters/Pilar Olivares

Key: t = top, b = bottom, c = center, l = left, r = right, sp = single page, dp = double page

All other photos are from Ripley Entertainment Inc.
Every attempt has been made to acknowledge correctly and contact copyright holders and we apologize in advance for any unintentional errors or omissions, which will be corrected in future editions.